Big 4 Accounting Firms Interview Questions

32 Questions & Answers To Get You The Big 4 Job You Dese----

By Christian V

Copyright © 2017
big4accountingfirms.com
All Rights Reserved

CHAPTER ONE
Why You Need This Book

Are you going through the big 4 interview process right now? Do you have any idea what the big 4 are going to be asking you? It's ok if you don't, because this book will provide over 30 interview questions and answers to help you get ready. This book was written by the same team behind **big4accountingfirms.com** and **The Big 4 Accounting Firms Recruiting Guide** ebook on Amazon.

We are excited to be helping you on your big four journey. You should be excited too. You are going to be working for one of the largest professional services firms in the world. If you picture yourself getting that big 4 job and use this book to help with the interview, you have a great chance at getting the big 4 career that you deserve.

In addition to big 4 interview questions that you will be asked, this book offers questions that **you can ask** your big 4 recruiter and a **free resume template** at the end of the book.

The format of the book is to:

- First provide you with the question that will be asked in the interview.
- Then we provide the reason around why the big 4 ask

that question.
- Then we give what a bad answer would be to the questions,
- and finally what a good answer would be.
- We also provide reasoning behind why an answer is good or bad.
- Each question is categorized into a skill/chapter that the big 4 will test you on based on the interview question.

The reason we formatted the book this way is to help you understand the types of questions that you will be asked and why you are being asked those questions. There are too many times where I have interviewed candidates, and they answered with an inappropriate answer. They didn't respond inappropriately because they weren't intelligent or bad people. They responded inappropriately because they didn't practice or no one taught them how to interview.

You don't need to have the same problems when you interview with the big 4 because this book will help you get inside the big 4 interview process. You will understand the types of questions that you will be asked. You will also understand the types of answers to avoid and the types of answers that will make you a superior candidate.

Some people can't come up with interview answers themselves because they aren't good interviewers. This book will help you come up with examples if you can't think of any yourself. It will begin to jog your memory and get you into the optimal big 4 interviewee mindset.

CHAPTER TWO
Introduction

Welcome to the big 4 accounting firms interview questions. You have likely bought this book because you have an interview coming up and want to find out all the questions that you will be asked. You are already on track to make it to the big 4. Being prepared is one of the most important things to performing well at the big 4.

Some words of caution before we get started. I know that you want to know all the possibilities of questions that you will be asked. Don't try to memorize the exact questions and the answers in this book. Doing that will not do you any good.

We've broken this book down into categories to get you to think about why you are being asked the questions. This will also help you brainstorm about the answers that you will provide to the big 4. You need to start brainstorming now. What do we mean by brainstorming? Well it's assessing the stories of your life and understanding how those fit into the big 4 story.

The big 4 wants to assess your past behavior to see how it will fit into their culture. As you read through this book read why the big 4 ask these questions, and then reflect back on various aspects of your life to see how they fit together.

Keep a notepad with you throughout the day. Start scribbling down how your story fits into the big 4 story. If you read this book and do that exercise as well, you will be more prepared than the vast majority of other candidates.

What are some good ideas for where you can get your stories from? Use your experiences at other jobs, in school projects, in team sports or in other activities.

We've listed out some ideas below:

Past Jobs

Don't be afraid to use past jobs as answers to big 4 questions. Most people that interview with the big 4 at an entry-level candidate level have never had jobs before the big 4. If you have the experience, use it.

Now let's get to areas of your past jobs where you should start focusing your memory. Try to remember

When you've worked in teams (increasing sales, teaching others to use a cash register)
When you've communicated really
Taken on responsibility (Watched store without a manager)

CHAPTER THREE
Ability to Face Change

One of the most important things in the Big 4 Accounting Firms is the ability to face change. Everything happens at a rapid pace in the Big 4, so if you can't face change you'll be out of the job. The big 4 will test you in your interview to make sure you can face change.

The Big 4 will assess whether you meet the following criteria to see whether you can face change

1. Maintain focus - can you maintain your focus in a constantly changing environment.

2. Understand change - In order to adapt to change you have to first be able to understand it. Can you understand changes in tasks, situations and environments as well as the logic for the change.

3. Cope effectively - Can you strategize and adapt to altering conditions and avoid stress.

4. Adjust behavior - The big 4 will test your ability to modify your behavior to deal effectively with changes.

Interview Question 1

We all have to make changes when the way we've been doing things is no longer effective. Tell me about a time when you've had to try a new approach to a task. What did you do? What were the results?

Why do they ask this question?

The big 4 ask this question because they want to know if you can reassess your thinking. If your approach is incorrect, do you have the ability to see that and adjust, or will you just stay on your current course. In the big 4, you have to be able to admit defeat and change your approach.

Bad Answer

An example of a bad answer to this question would be:

I once had a group project where someone on my team disagreed with my way of thinking. I persisted and stated that my point of view was the correct one until they came around to my way of thinking.

Why is this a bad answer: You want to show how you changed your way of thinking and not the other way around. One of the biggest parts of maturing and becoming a good business person is viewing things from another person's viewpoint.

Good Answer

An example of a good answer to this question would be:

I had a group project in school where I tried to do a majority of the work because of communication gaps within the group. I quickly realized I could not complete the project by myself and opened different lines of communication with my group. I was able to communicate effectively and coordinate with my team members to get the project completed in a timely manner.

<u>Why this is a good answer</u>:

This shows how you had one way of thinking but saw the flaw in that thinking. You then reassessed your position on the fly and adapted. You also adapted to work in a team which is another benefit of this answer.

Interview Question 2

Tell me about a situation in which you had to adjust quickly to a significant change at school or work. How did the change affect you? What did you do?

Why do they ask this question

The big 4 ask this question to understand how you will respond to significant changes on the job. The big 4 are well known for high turnover, so they want to make sure you won't freak out when your superior or colleagues leave the job. The firm might also lose a significant client, and you might have to change to a different group. In conclusion, the big 4 are constantly facing change and you must be willing to adapt in order to succeed.

Bad Answer

<u>An example of a bad answer to this question would be</u>:

I once worked at a restaurant where a lot of the people quit during a high pressure time at the restaurant. I made sure to isolate myself and focus on my work to make sure that I did everything correctly. I didn't want to let my environment affect my way of thinking.

<u>Why is this a bad answer</u>:

Even though you showed that you were able to focus on your work, you also showed that you didn't think about the team at all. This shows that you aren't team-oriented and look to help yourself.

Good Answer

<u>An example of a good answer to this question would be</u>:

I once worked at a store where all of my colleagues quit around the same time to go back to their respective colleges. This caused a big change at the store and was hectic for the store owner. I went to the store owner and asked him if he needed help, and if I should take on more responsibility.

He thanked me and said that there were more things I could help him with. I took on more responsibility and helped the owner out. I also even ended up referring some of my other friends that didn't go to college for jobs with that store.

<u>Why this is a good answer</u>:

This shows how you didn't fear the change that occurred. You saw the change occur and then you calculated your next move. It was a good move too because it helped someone other than yourself. This is the type of action that the big 4 accounting firms want to see out of the best candidates.

Interview Question 3

Describe a time when your workload in school was unusually heavy. How did you respond?

Why do they ask this question

If you have done any research on the big four public accounting firms, then you understand why they might be asking this question. They ask this question because you will undoubtedly face a huge workload when you work for the big 4. They want to see whether you have ever faced a significant workload before and how you faced it.

Bad Answer

An example of a bad answer to this question would be:

I had a very large workload at the beginning of a semester at school. I understood that I couldn't handle that course workload, so I dropped a class.

Why is this a bad answer:

This isn't necessarily a bad answer in everyday life. This is a bad answer for the big 4. You obviously knew your limitations and called the quits when you faced them, but that is not what the big 4 want to see. They want to hear about situations where you faced extreme workloads and then problem solved your way out of it.

Good Answer

An example of a good answer to this question would be:

I once had school projects due in all my classes at college, so

I needed to come up with a plan to complete all the projects. At the time, I was doing a lot of extracurricular sporting activities. I decided to cut back on those activities until all my projects were completed to the best of my abilities.

After my projects were done, I resumed my extracurricular activities because I enjoyed them and because I enjoyed spending time with my friends.

<u>Why this is a good answer</u>:

This shows how you didn't fold in the face of extra work. You assessed your current workload and your personal life and you prioritized. This is also a good answer because you showed that you resumed the personal activities that meant the most to you. The big 4 would be impressed by this because many of them have big worklife balance initiatives. They don't like to see people become workaholics anymore. You have to show the ability to balance work and personal life.

CHAPTER FOUR
Learning At Work

Another thing the big 4 want to assess is whether you can learn at work. Some people can work 30 years in their career and learn nothing new. They just do the same low level work everyday and never learn or move up. This is not the type of person the big 4 want to hire. That is why the big 4 will assess whether or not you can learn on the job.

Interview Question 4

What did you learn from your (fill in the blank) experience at school or work? How did you use this learning elsewhere?

Why do they ask this question

The big 4 ask this question to see how you learned from an experience at school or experience at work. They will likely ask you this type of question after you tell them a story about your school life or work life.

Bad Answer

An example of a bad answer to this question would be:

I once had a job at a ticket office at my school's football

stadium. I really learned my responsibilities, so much so that I could zone out a little bit. I could go a whole day working with a lot of customers without having to be really engaged.

<u>Why is this a bad answer</u>:

This might be an extreme example, but I show it for a reason. You don't want to show how you learn the minimal amount necessary. You really want to show how you can constantly learn throughout your job or whatever you are doing.

Good Answers

<u>An example of a good answer to this question would be:</u>

While in school I took many excel classes to make me more efficient on my school projects. I later obtained a part time job as a bookkeeper. I was able to utilize the excel skills I learned in school to help me be a successful bookkeeper.

<u>Why this is a good answer</u>:

This shows how you used something you learned in school to a real-life job. It takes some actual thought to implement something you learn in a school environment to the outside world. If you can show a direct example of how you did this, that is a great advantage over other candidates.

Interview Question 5

What was the most difficult course you took in school? How

did you master it?

Why do they ask this question

The big 4 ask this question because they want to see how you handle difficult topics and situations. Financial accounting consists of concepts that are hard to master. Your clients might also be smart and difficult to deal with. In order to succeed at the big 4 you need to be able to deal with difficult subject matter and difficult people.

Bad Answer

I found math hard because I don't like math. I mastered math by studying with someone that liked math. Then I made sure to never take a math class again.

Why this is a bad answer:

This is a bad answer because it shows that the candidate isn't willing to face difficult situations. You need to have a story behind everything. You can't just have short succinct answers or negative answers.

Good Answer

An example of a good answer to this question would be:

The most difficult course I took in school was intermediate accounting. It was difficult because we were required to utilize all the accounting knowledge we acquired in school to financial statement concepts.

I mastered the subject matter by spending more time than I had ever spent studying. I also went to more study groups and teachers sessions. I did this to make sure that I utilized all resources necessary to help me succeed in the class.

<u>Why this is a good answer</u>:

This answer shows that the candidate exhausted all resources to master a subject that they found difficult. The big 4 want to be able to see that you are willing to go to great lengths to answer difficult questions and please difficult people.

Interview Question 6

When learning a new subject in school, we pick up some things quickly, while other subjects take more time to learn. Tell me about a subject you learned quickly and one that took you a bit more time. How did your approach to the more difficult subject differ from your approach to the easier one?

Why do they ask this question

The big 4 ask this question because they want to see how you handle difficult topics and situations. Financial accounting consists of concepts that are hard to master. Your clients might also be very smart and impatient with slow learners. This might make them difficult to deal with at first. In order to succeed at the big 4 you need to be able to deal with difficult subject matter and difficult people.

Bad Answer

Accounting was super easy for me in school while computer science was not easy. I dealt with accounting by not spending much time on it. I approached the more difficult subject by leaning on my computer science lab groups. I was fortunate because computer science was primarily a group-based class.

Why this is a bad answer:

This doesn't show how you dealt with a difficult situation. It just shows how you lean on others to get your hard work done.

Good Answer

An example of a good answer to this question would be:

One class that was easy for me in school was tax research. Research came naturally to me because I love using google and other online research tools. I was able to use that knowledge of google and translate it to the tax research tools that we had at my school.

One subject that was more difficult to me was advanced accounting. I had to approach it much more differently than tax research. I had to motivate myself to study for advanced accounting because I didn't like it. I did this by providing rewards to myself for studying a certain amount of time. I didn't have to give myself much incentive in the tax research class because it came naturally to me.

Why this is a good answer:

This is a good answer because it provides one area where you struggled and one area where you succeeded. It also shows how you took different approaches to each. This example also shows how you were aware enough to realize that you need to motivate yourself in order to get better results.

Interview Question 7

Describe how you identified and pursued learning

opportunities in new areas.

Why do they ask this question

The big 4 ask this question to make sure that you are actually interested in learning. If you aren't interested in learning, then you won't have a good story about how you pursued new learning opportunities.

Bad Answer

I liked accounting, so I decided to major in accounting at school.

Why this is a bad answer: You don't want to show how you followed a set path for learning. You want to show you went above and beyond.

Good Answer

An example of a good answer to this question would be:

I heard from friends at school that excel was very important for an accounting internship, so I decided to pursue additional learning opportunities to get better at excel. My college offered some voluntary courses on excel that I took advantage of. I also utilized online learning courses and youtube to become better at Excel.

Why this is a good answer: This answer shows that you pursued learning opportunities other than those set out in front of you. It shows that you are willing to go to great lengths to learn. It is often hard to find time to learn at the big 4. You have to show the initiative to be willing to learn.

CHAPTER FIVE
Are You Courageous?

You have to demonstrate courage at the big 4. You can't just be a weak wallflower. You will face very tough situations. What does the big 4 consider as having courage and integrity? The following would be measures of courage and integrity.

- Takes positive action - Do you resolve issues in a way that dissipates conflict and maintains relationships?
- Responds quickly - Do you take immediate action when problems occur?
- Demonstrate integrity - Can you deal with people in a forthright manner?
- Behave consistently - Are your words and actions consistent? Do you behave consistently; even with difficult individuals?

Interview Question 8

Have you ever taken an unpopular stand on a topic in school? What was the situation and what did you do?

Why do they ask this question

This is a tricky question, and it must be handled delicately. The big 4 are trying to see if you are willing to push back if you believe something is wrong or unethical.

They ask this because you will often face people on the job who are wrong and have to be willing to push back. In accounting, there is also a chance that you run into unethical situations that you will have to stand up against.

Bad Answer
An example of a bad answer to this question would be:

In school, I was a republican and let everyone know about it. Most people in school were liberals so it was a difficult stance to take.

Why this is a bad answer: You don't want to get political in an interview because you risk offending the interviewer.

Good Answer

An example of a good answer to this question would be:

In school, I took a class on corporate income tax. In that class we had to prepare a schedule M3 for a corporate income tax return. I felt that my preparation and categorization of certain items of income and deductions were correct. The teacher disagreed with me, but I spent time with the teacher to explain my logic. The teacher ended up understanding why I had prepared the form the way I did and awarded me credit.

Why this is a good answer: This answer shows that you were willing to go against the grain to stand up for something you believed was correct.

Interview Question 9

Tell me about a time when you felt a peer demonstrated inappropriate behavior. What happened? What did you do?

Why do they ask this question

Again the big 4 are testing your courage here. They want to see how you will act in the face of unethical behavior. Part of being a certified public accountant is protecting the public financial markets.

Bad Answer

An example of a bad answer to this question would be:

In school, I knew that one of my class mates had obtained a previous test and utilized it to get a high score on the current year's test. I was offered an opportunity to utilize the test, but I didn't do so.

Why this is a bad answer: This shows how you didn't stand up to or report inappropriate behavior. The big 4 expect you to report bad behavior to uphold the CPA designation and to protect their liability.

Good Answer

An example of a good answer to this question would be:

I saw a peer in one of my college courses cheating on a test once. The student was blatantly copying answers off of another student in class. After class, I brought the issue up to a professor. The school investigated and found that the student had indeed cheated on the test.

Why this is a good answer:

This shows that you saw something wrong and did something about it. This is what the big four want to see out of a candidate. They want their candidates to be courageous and stand up for what it is right. Not only because it is the right thing to do but also to limit their professional liability.

Interview Question 10

Give me an example of time when you proactively generated ideas or suggestions. What did you do? What happened as a result?

Why do they ask this question

The big 4 ask this question because they don't want people that are just going to sit back and chill at their desk. They want people that aren't afraid of being proactive and generating ideas on client projects.

In audit, they want you to come with ideas to make audits more efficient.

As you move up the chain of command, they want you to be more proactive in engaging clients and coming up with client projects.

Bad Answer

An example of a bad answer to this question would be:

During a group school project, I helped generate ideas with my fellow group mates.

Why this is a bad answer:

This doesn't show how you proactively generated ideas or suggestions. It just shows that you think coming up with a few ideas is ok. You need to be able to show how you generate ideas and how those ideas make a difference.

Good Answer

An example of a good answer to this question would be:

I worked part time during school. There was a process at my job that was consistently inefficient and resulted in 15 minute wait times for our customers. I thought the wait time for the customer could be reduced to 5 minutes or less. Therefore, I came up with an enhanced process and suggested it to my supervisor.

My supervisor took it into consideration and later implemented it. The enhanced process helped reduce wait times to less than 5 minutes.

Why this is a good answer:

This shows how you proactively generated an idea that actually provided results to a business. It is also detailed and to the point.

Interview Question 10

We've all had close friends or classmates come to us for help on assignments/projects they were expected to complete on their own. Can you tell me about a time when this happened to you? How did you respond?

Why do they ask this question

This is another tricky question that the big 4 are likely to ask to see how you respond to being assigned work.

This question is also very important in light of recent worklife balance measures. You have to be able to show that you don't just say yes to everything. You have to be able to show courage. It might be hard to say no or to suggest work be given to someone else, but it is necessary in order to be successful at the Big 4.

Bad Answer

An example of a bad answer to this question would be:

Whenever someone asks me to do something; I just do it.

Why this is a bad answer:

This is not an appropriate response. You need to show how you deal with situations where people ask you to do more than you can complete. There are also situations where people try to take advantage of you, and there are people that will try to do this over and over in the big 4. You need to show how you'd respond in that situation.

Good Answer

An example of a good answer to this question would be:

I used to have a friend in school that would find creative ways of asking me to do his work. It would usually be asking for help, and then he'd ask me to show him how to do it. He'd do that over and over to see if I'd complete each task for him. I'd complete a couple of examples for him, but then I would switch it over to him. I would tell him that he needed to complete some tasks so that he could learn as well.

Why this is a good answer:

This shows how you don't let people roll over you when it comes to work. You had someone that tried to take advantage of you, and you dealt with it appropriately. You didn't blatantly call your friend out. You found a unique way to make sure that you weren't doing your work and his.

CHAPTER SIX
Project Management Skills

Another requirement for working at the big 4 is being able to effectively manage a project. The big four will want to see if you can efficiently plan and perform work in accordance with client and professional standards. Can you identify and address issues, problems and opportunities. Here are some key things that the big 4 will be looking for from an ideal candidate

- Prioritizes - Can you identify more critical and less critical activities and assignments.
- Determines tasks and resources - Can you determine project or assignment requirements by breaking them down into tasks and identify types of equipment, materials, and people needed.
- Schedules - Do you allocate appropriate amounts of time for completing your own and others' work.
- Leverage resources - Do you take advantage of available resources.

Interview Question 12

How did you balance your schoolwork with extracurricular activities?

Why do they ask this question

This question is asked because the big four want to see if you can balance work and life. There are also things outside of work that you have to attend. You can't just make an excuse that you are busy with work. Clients want to see you at events and so does big 4 leadership. You have to be social if you want to succeed at the big four.

Bad Answer

An example of a bad answer to this question would be:

I don't have time for extracurricular activities because I'm too busy with school.

Why this is a bad answer:

Everyone is busy. They have multiple jobs or have multiple things going on in life. You also have to remember that most big 4 partners have families. This means that they have to make time for work and their families. Because of this, you can't say that you only have time for school.

Good Answer

An example of a good answer to this question would be:

I make time for my extracurricular activities by scheduling out my study time every week. I also schedule out time to meet with teachers and teacher's assistants.

Why this is a good answer:

This shows how you are able to balance your schedule. It also shows how you don't just focus in one area of your life.

You balance your schoolwork with your extracurricular activities. In the big 4, partners no longer want to see people sacrifice their whole lives for accounting. There is more to life and partners realize that. Many of them will want you to have worklife balance. Practicing dealing with difficult work and having fun in school will help you in the workplace.

Interview Question 13

Tell me about a time when you faced conflicting priorities. How did you determine the top priority?

Why do they ask this question?

The big 4 ask this question because they want to assess your prioritization skills. At the big four, you have to be able to prioritize. There will be times where you have too much work. You won't be able to work on everything at once, and you won't be able to get all your work delegated out. When you face that type of situation, you will have to prioritize which task to complete first.

Bad Answer
An example of a bad answer to this question would be:

When I face conflicting priorities, I choose the item that came into my workflow first.

Why this is a bad answer:

First in, first out is a good concept for accounting, but it is not a good concept in prioritization. You don't want to give any kind of answer that represents first in first out. At the big 4 you will have many administrative tasks such as billing. You need to be able to put things like that to the side when there is client work to be completed.

Good Answer

An example of a good answer to this question would be:

I once faced conflicting priorities at school with my course work. I had two assignments due on the same day. I prioritized which task to complete first based on several factors. I first looked at how long it would take to complete each task. I determined that it would take about the same time for each task, so I went to the next factor.

I next looked at which task I was the most motivated to complete, and I decided to do that task later. If I was motivated to work on the task, then I wouldn't need much energy to work on it. I decided this because I knew that both tasks would require a lot of work. If I left the task that I was less motivated to complete until later, then there was a chance that I would be tired and wouldn't complete it until closer to the deadline.

Why this is a good answer:

This shows your thought process around prioritization. It shows how you gave a lot of thought to multiple prioritization factors.

Interview Question 14

We've all been in situations in which we couldn't complete everything we needed to do on time. Tell me about a time when this happened to you.

Why do they ask this question?

This is another scary question. Why do the big four ask this question? They ask this because you will actually face situations in the big 4 where you won't have enough time to complete tasks. You might even miss deadlines because of this, but that is obviously not the situation you want to run into.

Bad Answer

There was a time where I was supposed to complete a project for school, and I didn't have enough time to complete it. I just did the best job that I could and handed in a project that wasn't the best that I could do. I was able to complete the project but not in the way I would have liked to.

<u>Why this is a bad answer</u>:

You don't want to admit that you completed a project without giving a 100%. You actually don't want to show too much weakness in an interview at all. I know that no one is perfect, but an interview is all about perception. You also don't want to say that you used an excuse to get an extension on a deadline. This seems unethical.

Good Answer

<u>An example of a good answer to this question would be</u>:

I realized that I was not going to meet a deadline at school because of some personal reasons that came up. Luckily I noticed this in advance and was able to explain my problem to the professor. The professor understood and gave me a one day extension which enabled me to turn in my project with 100% confidence.

Why this is a good answer:

You want to show that you knew you were going to miss the deadline. This shows your ability to manage a project. It also shows that you are willing to have a tough conversation in order to deliver a good product.

You have to be willing to have tough conversations with clients in order to be successful at the big 4. Clients can sometimes be scary and mean. If you aren't afraid to have tough conversations, you will be seen as an asset at the big four.

Interview Question 15

Walk me through a situation in which you asked questions of several people for the information you needed to make an effective decision. How did you know who and what to ask?

Why do they ask this question?

The big 4 want to see if you a deep thinker because that is what is required of an auditor and/or a consultant. You can't always assume things are a certain way. Sometimes you need to ask questions to learn more about a situation or a transaction. A lot of people in the big four get into a mind-frame where they just follow what was done last year. That is not what the big 4 want from a future employee. They want someone that is thoughtful and willing to ask deep questions.

Bad Answer

I was making a decision about which college to attend. In order to make my decision I polled all my friends about which school was the coolest. I decided to go to the school that everyone thought was the most popular.

<u>Why this is a bad answer</u>:

Even though you asked multiple people in this scenario it was not asking for good information. It was also a "go with the flow" mentality which is not what you should highlight in a big 4 interview.

Good Answer

<u>An example of a good answer to this question would be</u>:

When I was investigating what major to choose in college, I asked multiple people about what major to choose. I actually asked many people. I knew that I likely wanted to be an engineer or an accountant. I asked people questions about pay, ability to move up and career progression. I eventually learned from multiple people that accounting opens up many doors in the business world, and I liked business. Therefore, based on my personality and the answers I got from the people that I asked, I chose to go with accounting as my major.

<u>Why this is a good answer</u>:

It shows that you put thought into your decision and your questions. It also showed that you asked multiple sources when investigating your decision. Even after you asked all your sources, you still came back and measured those answers against your internal assumptions. You want to seem thoughtful when asked a question a like this so try to think of a good example beforehand.

CHAPTER SEVEN
Can You Focus on Your Client

You most likely know that the big 4 are client facing professionals. This means that you will need the ability to focus on your clients. The big 4 will ask you certain interview questions to test whether you are able to do this. The questions that they will ask you will aim to assess your ability to:

- Seek to understand clients - Can you actively seek information to understand clients' circumstances, problems, and needs.
- Do you try to educate clients - Do you share information and knowledge materials with your clients to build their understanding of issues and capabilities.
- Can you build collaborative relationships with your clients - This entails being able to build rapport and cooperative relationships with your clients.
- Do you delivery quality to your clients - This entails delivering work of the highest standards of excellence.
- Do you have client feedback systems - Are systems in place to monitor and evaluate client concerns?

Interview Question 16

Tell me about a time when it was important to understand the requirements of your professor for a particular assignment.

What did you do to better understand those requirements?

Why do they ask this question?

The big 4 want to see if you will truly listen to your clients. There are many clients who don't provide the full picture upon the first meeting. They know what they want, but they don't necessarily know how to provide that detail to you. Because of that you have to be willing to go to great lengths to understand them. You have to be willing to ask questions not only of them, but also of your team members who have been on the client for some time. You also need to do research on your own sometimes.

This question could also relate to others on your team. Senior associates and managers in the big 4 work long hours and have been doing the work for a number of years. They don't necessarily remember every step necessary to complete a given project. Because of this, you need to be willing to go to great lengths to understand your assignment before you start. Otherwise you might be inefficient in completing the project and make it go over budget.

Bad Answer

An example of a bad answer to this question would be:

I was once given a tough assignment at school and the professor wasn't too clear on what the criteria for the assignment were. I used my own knowledge of the teacher to surmise what was required of the assignment, and I ended up getting a good grade.

Why this is a bad answer:

Even though you might have received a good grade, you didn't show the lengths that you went to get a better understanding. What made the criteria hard to understand? You also need to show what lengths you went to get a better understanding. You don't necessarily need to show that you asked the professor, but you need to be able to describe in detail how far you went to get an understanding.

Good Answer

An example of a good answer to this question would be:

There was a particular assignment in my tax class where one of my professors stated that there were no "right" answers on the project. She stated that we just needed to support our answers. Based on my interactions with this professor, I knew that there was a certain way she wanted this assignment completed. She was a very particular professor.

In order to better understand the needs for the assignment, I went to her teacher hours and spent a great deal of time gaining an understanding on the assignment. I also spent time with her teachers assistant. By that time, I thought I had a good understanding of what was needed, but I wanted to check my thinking. To check my thought process, I even met with other students in the class to see if they had a similar understanding of the project. Only after I had gone through all these lengths to understand what was required of me on the project, did I begin my work.

Why this is a good answer:

This answer shows the rigor that you will go through to understand an assignment. This will give your big 4 interviewer comfort because they will know that you are willing to go to great lengths to understand a project. A senior associate or manager do not want to hold your hand through every project. Neither does a client for that case. You need to show that you have motivation to understand what is required of you on a given assignment.

Interview Question 17

How do you build collaborative relationships with peers and customers? Give me details about one or two of them.

Why do they ask this question?

You can't be isolated and work at the big 4. You have to be willing to collaborate in order to succeed. This question helps the big four understand if you can collaborate or if you isolate.

At the beginning of your career, you need to be able to go to your managers when you have questions. You also need to be able to interact with your peers in order to get tasks completed. There are many projects that have multiple staff people on them. Managers and partners don't want those staff working in silos and being isolated. They want them to speak and collaborate to provide the optimal value to the client and the team.

Bad Answer

An example of a bad answer to this question would be:

I really build my best relationships by being happy and smiling a lot. I try to be as nice as possible so that everyone likes me.

<u>Why this is a bad answer</u>:

You can't just say that you naturally build relationships because it does not provide insight. You also can't say that you aren't good at relationships at all. You need to provide some insight into how you build collaborative relationships. Even if you can't think of someone you have built a collaborative relationship with, come up with a fictional character or a pet and just rename that character or pet to a person.

Good Answer

<u>An example of a good answer to this question would be</u>:

When I worked in retail, I used to ask customers if they needed help. If they said yes, I would ask detailed questions about their needs so that I could better help them. I was truly interested in their needs so that I could help them and so that I could progress as a retail professional.

If they said they did not need help, I would tell them to let me know if they ever wanted help and then I left them alone. I did this because I know that some people want to accomplish tasks alone and need time to think before asking for help.

<u>Why this is a good answer</u>:

This answer shows how you really had a method to collaborating with your customers. It also shows how you considered not only extroverted customers but introverted ones as well. Many accountants are very introverted, and you will need to be able to build collaborative relationships with them as well.

Interview Question 18

What have you done to understand a peer's or customer's point of view?

Why do they ask this question?

The big 4 ask this question because it is very common for people to focus on themselves and not others. The big 4 do not want this type of candidate because the big 4 are client facing. You always have to look out for the best interest of the client. You can't be selfish and always worried about yourself.

Bad Answer

An example of a bad answer to this question would be:

I try to look at other people's point of view when I work with them. I try to be considerate and nice. I want to treat them like I would want them to treat me.

Why this is a bad answer:

It doesn't show the steps you've taken to see the other person's point of view. It is nice that you try to treat people how you want to be treated, but that is not enough in this case. You need to be able to describe a situation where you considered another person's point of view and how you did that.

Good Answer

An example of a good answer to this question would be:

I was once working in a group in college and disagreed with one of my group members. I thought I was right, but I knew I needed to give the group person a shot in case they had a more efficient approach. I ended up listening to their viewpoint and wasn't convinced at first. After listening for a while I agreed with their approach. Their approach would be able to get us better grades and let us work more efficiently, so I ended up agreeing with them and implementing their approach.

<u>Why this is a good answer</u>:

This is a good approach for many reasons. It shows how you disagreed with the approach at first.

It was great that you show you disagreed and were still able to come around on the idea. You would not have been able to come around to the idea without being able to consider the other person's viewpoint.

CHAPTER EIGHT
Building Relationships

Another thing that the big 4 want to see from ideal candidates is the ability to build and sustain relationships. You need to be able to grow and sustain relationships through development of internal and external networks. They want to know if you can perform the following functions:

- Can you identify relationship needs - Can you analyze the organization and identify key relationships that should be initiated or improved?
- Do you explore relationship opportunities - Do you exchange information with others to clarify relationship benefits and potential problems?
- Do you monitor relationships - Can you implement effective means of monitoring and evaluating the relationship process?
- Do you formulate action plans - Do you collaboratively determine courses of action to realize mutual goals?

Interview Question 19

Tell me about a time when you had to reach out to others with whom you were unfamiliar for assistance. What did you do?

Why do they ask this question?

This is a great question for entry-level candidates. I say that because this was one of my greatest fears coming into the big 4. I asked myself, "Am I really going to have to deal with people all day long?"

The answer is yes you will. The big 4 want to see if you are willing to speak to people. They want to see if you are able to reach out to clients for document requests. They also want to see if you are able to reach out to specialists within the firm. In conclusion, you have to be able to reach out when you need something or don't know something. The big 4 want to see if you are already doing that in your life.

Bad Answer

An example of a bad answer to this question would be:

At my job I had to reach out to my supervisor for help. I didn't fully understand how to use the software at my bookkeeping job.

Why this is a bad answer:

This is a bad answer for multiple reasons. First off you already knew your supervisor. The question was reaching out to somebody that you did not fully know. Second you didn't really ask for that much assistance. You just asked for a little bit of help with software.

Good Answer

An example of a good answer to this question would be:

At my bookkeeping job, we started using some new bookkeeping software. I asked the owner of the bookkeeping business for assistance, however; she did not know how to teach me the software.

Therefore, I had to reach out to the software company directly on multiple occasions. I ended up establishing a good relationship with the software vendor. So much so that I became a specialist in the software. They even labeled me as a local champion in the software. They asked me to help some of their other clients understand how their software could help them at trade shows and conventions. This increased my exposure to the accounting community in my city. I would not have received this exposure if I was not willing to reach out to the software vendor directly for further assistance.

Why this is a good answer:

Do you see how this one is a better answer? Although the problem is the same with the software, you actually end up coming up with a better solution to the problem. You also showed how you got there. This answer shows how you didn't just stop at your supervisor when you didn't get the right answer. You went the extra step and reached out to the software vendor themselves. This shows how you are willing to go that extra mile to get the right answer.

Interview Question 20

Give me an example of using your personal network of friends and acquaintances help you accomplish a task.

Why do they ask this question?

The reason the big four ask this question is because it's important to use your network. The big four accounting firms love the word network. No one is a network. The network is just a group of your friends and acquaintances that is why they're asking the question this way. You have to show how you aren't afraid to ask your friends for help.

Bad Answer

An example of a bad answer to this question would be:

I once asked my friend if his dad to get me a job at their restaurant. My friend wasn't able to help me, but he did suggest another restaurant for me to work at.

Why this is a bad answer:

This doesn't show how you work with your friends to accomplish a task. All this shows that you can ask your friend for a simple favor, and your friend wasn't able to accomplish it. It makes it seem like you don't know how to ask the right questions because you did not achieve your goal. You want to show how you asked a question to your friend and succeeded.

Good Answer

An example of a good answer to this question would be:

In college, I volunteered at a homeless shelter. Part of my volunteer work was helping with fundraising. There was a particular event the homeless shelter was hosting where I had a fundraising goal. In order to meet this goal, I had to reach out to family members, friends, and acquaintances. I had to provide a detailed description of my tasks at this volunteer center in order to raise as much money as possible. Through my communication and collaboration with my friends, I was able to raise enough money to meet my goal and even surpassed it.

<u>Why this is a good answer</u>:

This answer is a good answer for multiple reasons. Not only are you answering the question thoroughly, but you are also showing that you care about your community. You showed a task, volunteer work, that you were working towards. You also showed that you worked with your friends and acquaintances to achieve that goal.

Interview Question 21

When have you help others around you without being asked? How did you know they needed your help?

Why do they ask this question?

This is another question where the big four accounting firms went to see how far you're willing to go in order to meet client needs. If you are always waiting for your client to call you, then there this chance that another big four firm will steal your work. You have to show how you are constantly aware of your client's needs.

Bad Answer

<u>An example of a bad answer to this question would be:</u>

I once gave a homeless person some change.

<u>Why this is a bad answer</u>:

Although giving a homeless person change is something that a good Samaritan with you, it's not a good example for this purpose. You need to show through your description how do you observed a need in somebody without them knowing.

Good Answer

An example of a good answer to this question would be:

In high school I had a friend that was deathly afraid of writing an essay for the college admission process. I kept asking him if he needed help and he kept saying no.

As time passed, I could see that he was becoming more and more stressed. One day I took him out for a cup of coffee, and I asked him, "please let me help you." That is when he finally said yes. Me and him ended up going to the library and working on his essay for hours until we got it just right. He ultimately ended up getting into the college of his dreams.

Why this is a good answer:

What this answer shows is that you observed something without being explicitly told. You also acted upon that feeling.

This is exactly what the big four accounting firms one from a candidate. They want a candidate who can observe the needs of the client without the client always blatantly asked. They want you to be available to observe the little things that are wrong with the client. Are they stressed out during busy season. Are they stressed out when it's not busy season?

These might be signs that your client really needs help. Maybe they just don't know how to ask for help. Maybe I'll have the money to hire you to help them. Maybe they need help asking their CFO for money to hire help.

CHAPTER NINE
Team Success

Another big 4 essential is working in teams. In order to make partner or get promoted at the big 4, you will have to work successfully in teams. This can be internal teams or in teams with the client. You will also have to work in teams with other specialist groups. You can't just isolate and work by yourself if you want to be successful at the big 4. The big four public accounting firms will test your ability to work in teams by testing the following skill areas:

- Can embrace shared values and goals - Can you demonstrate leadership and commitment to organizational shared values and goals?
- Do you open discussions effectively - Can you describe expectations, goals and requests in a way that provides clarity and excites interest?
- Can you facilitate agreement - This entails using appropriate influence strategies (such as demonstrating benefits or providing rewards).
- Can you clarify the situation - Can you give clear information that ensures that the situation is understood by team members?

Interview Question 22

Describe a time when you had to convince a fellow student or peer to use a particular approach to an assignment. What did you say?

Why do they ask this question?

Not all of your team members will know the best approach to a particular project. You need to be able to convince them of the right approach. They might also lack the knowledge of how to do it the right way. Therefore, you have to be willing to show them the right way without making them look like fools. There might also be situations where both your approaches are right, but your approach will get the team there faster and more efficiently. Efficiency is the key to success in the big four accounting firms.

Bad Answer

I had a part-time job at a fast food restaurant one summer after school. That summer I found a way to get my line of customers moving efficiently because of a few tricks I knew on the register. One of my colleagues always had a long line with his customers yelling at him. I raised my voice and told him to learn to be more efficient. I couldn't understand why he couldn't learn the same tricks on the register that I had. It seemed simple to me.

Why this is a bad answer:

Although this shows how you operated in the team at your restaurant, it doesn't show how you contributed to team success. It just shows how you were successful yet your coworker was not. You didn't seem interested in taking the time to help him learn. You need to show how you worked in a team and ultimately achieved success through an approach that you initiated.

Good Answer

An example of a good answer to this question would be:

In college I once had a computer science class. In that class, we were given a group project where we had to code a project. During that group project, we were having a lot of difficulty coming up with a solution. Therefore, I suggested that we break up pieces of the project for each of us to solve.

One of my group members disagreed with this approach. They thought it was better if we all worked on the solution together all at one time. I didn't necessarily disagree with this approach, but I knew we would finish the project on time if we took this approach.

I told my group member that we would not finish the project by the deadline if we all worked on it at the same time. I told them that in order for all of us to be successful we had to break the project up. The group member ultimately ended up seeing my side of the argument. We split the project up, then we ended up finishing it by the deadline.

Why this is a good answer:

This is a good answer because it shows how you disagreed with a group member, but you still came to a compromise. It also shows the steps you took to get to that compromise which shows your thoughtfulness.

Interview Question 23

Describe a time when you had to work with a team to

complete a project. What role did you play? What actions did you take to influence the outcome of your assignment?

Why do they ask this question?

The big 4 ask this question to understand how you work in a group. They want to see if you are an active participant or just a follower. They also want to see if you step into the leader role. If you do take a leadership role, are you overbearing. Do you take on too much responsibility?

Bad Answer

<u>An example of a bad answer to this question would be</u>:

I once did a science project in high school. My group wasn't filled with the brightest people, so I just took the project over. We ended getting an A because I took over and dominated the project.

<u>Why this is a bad answer</u>:

This just shows that you aren't willing to trust group members and that you are judgmental. You need to show the ability to work with people of all different types of skill-sets. You can't say that you only work with the best and brightest. That makes you seem judgmental and cocky.

Good Answer

<u>An example of a good answer to this question would be</u>:

I once had a very big group project in my advanced accounting class. There were multiple parts that had to be tackled. I was co-leader with another classmate, and we both assessed everyone's likes and dislikes and doled out responsibilities based on that. We assigned someone to research who liked to research. We assigned someone to lead the oral presentation who loved communicating. We delegated the remaining responsibilities in a similar manner. The group got along well and our final presentation was a great success. Our presentation was the most popular in the whole classroom.

Why this is a good answer:

This really shows how you work well in a team environment. You immediately jumped into the lead role and used that to help the team as a whole and not yourself.
You assessed everyone's strengths and weaknesses and delegated workloads based on that.

Interview Question 24

Describe a situation when you had to influence another student or peer to cooperate. What did you say?

Why do they ask this question?

The big 4 want to see how you deal with uncooperative people or just how you get people to see your viewpoint.I think they ask this to see how you deal with uncooperative people because that is a common scenario that you will run into when you work at the big 4 accounting firms. There are many associates that come in with bad attitudes or think that they are too smart to listen to directions. You have to learn how to break through to these type of candidates.

Bad Answer

An example of a bad answer to this question would be:

I once had an uncooperative group member in my intermediate accounting class. In order to get him to cooperate told him to improve his attitude or else. He said that he didn't want to cooperate. Then I told him that I was going to tell the professor if you cooperate. We ended up switching group members to address the issue.

Why this is a bad answer:

This is a bad answer because it shows that you used threats to get what you want. Instead you want to show how you can work with almost any person. You want to show how late you convince someone to come to your side. You don't want to show how you always result to threats. That's what children do.

Good Answer

An example of a good answer to this question would be:

I once had a roommate in college who was very noisy. I asked him multiple times to turn down his music. When that didn't work, I had come up with a different solution.

I ended up sitting down with him and telling him how difficult it was to deal with his noise. I told them how I would really appreciate it if you could keep the noise level to a minimum so that I could study. I was willing to work with him so that he could still listen to his music. I worked out a schedule of when he could play his music so that I could maximize my study time. He would listen to his music while I was at class. This worked out really well for us and we avoided future conflict

Why this is a good answer:

This is a good answer because it shows how you avoid a conflict. You could have yelled at your roommate or threatened him but you didn't. Instead you came up with the common solution. You didn't lose your temper. It shows that you are really interested in coming to compromise as opposed to just looking out for yourself.

Interview Question 25

What techniques have you used to gain acceptance of ideas or plans? Give me an example of a time when you used one of these techniques.

Why do they ask this question?

The big four ask this question to understand how you convince other people of your ideas and plans. That is they try to see if you even convince people at all. Maybe you don't do a lot of convincing, and you have a weakness in this area. That's what they're trying to figure out.

Bad Answer

An example of a bad answer to this question would be:

I normally just mention my ideas as they come to me, and I truly hope that people adopt my idea after the first time I mention it. I might bring up the idea one more time, but I don't really push anything. I try being nice and calm and that's how I try to convince people.

Why this is a bad answer:

Even though this might be how most people communicate, it

doesn't make for good answer to this question. The best candidate that the big four want to see should have multiple skill sets to convince people of their ideas and plans. Now is that how people actually are? I don't think so, but you're going to want to make yourself seem that way to the big four.

Good Answer

An example of a good answer to this question would be:

I use multiple techniques to get people to implement my plans and ideas. I try to see things from their viewpoint before speaking to them. That way I don't offend them which will allow them to see things from my viewpoint.I also take people out for coffee, drinks, or even a meal. When you buy people things and listen to them, they are much more willing to support you.

I'm also an active listener. I listen very attentively when people speak to me and my responses are measured and to the point. I only speak when I feel I have something to contribute and whatever I say tends to be a positive response to what the person just said.

Another technique that I use, is that if I disagree with somebody's opinion is asking questions. I ask pointed questions to where I think the weaknesses in their argument are. The questions that I ask are not offensive though. By asking questions, I hopefully get the person to see the weaknesses in their argument.

Why this is a good answer:

You detailed all your techniques that you use to get your peers to cooperate. This is also a good answer because none of the techniques are negative. You want to have at least a couple positive techniques ready. If you have only one, it will make your interviewer doubt that you really have techniques for cooperation at all.

CHAPTER TEN
Can You Coach Others?

The ability to seek, provide and use timely feedback to help others and yourself improve is essential at the big 4. The big 4 will assess your following coaching skills throughout the interview process.

- Can you provide feedback and reinforcement - Can you give timely, constructive and appropriate feedback on performance? Can you reinforce other people's efforts and progress?
- Do you seek coaching - In your workflow, do you actively seek and use guidance from others to assist you in your personal development?
- Can you explain and demonstrate - Can you provide instruction, positive models, and opportunities for observation in order to help others.

Interview Question 26

Describe a recent coaching discussion you experienced where you were either the coach or the person being coached. What was the task? How did you involve the other person in the discussion?

Why do they ask this question?

In order to be successful at the big 4 or in business in general, you have to be willing to take feedback. Coaching is a form of feedback. Coaching and feedback are an everyday part of the big 4, so you have to show that you can take constructive feedback without getting offended or talking back.

Bad Answer

<u>An example of a bad answer to this question would be</u>:

I recently went to a resume workshop to have my resume reviewed, and there was coach present who was coaching me on how to improve my resume. Although I thought the person had some valid points, I felt that my resume was strong enough without their suggestions.

<u>Why this is a bad answer</u>:

It is a good answer in that it shows willingness to see a coach, but it also shows that you didn't listen to the coach once you received the feedback.

Good Answer

<u>An example of a good answer to this question would be</u>:

I recently attended a toastmasters session at my school which helps with public speaking. The task was to give a speech and effectively communicate my message. I gave a speech on a topic that I selected. I engaged the people in the session by asking them for feedback. I involved them by asking for their feedback and then listening intently to their feedback. In the next session, I implemented the majority of the feedback that I was provided.

<u>Why this is a good answer</u>:

This shows that you are open to feedback especially since you attended a session that was specifically focused on feedback. It is also good that this answer showed how the feedback was later implemented.

Interview Question 27

Tell me what you've done to help a peer understand what knowledge/skill areas to strengthen. Give me a specific example.

Why do they ask this question?

As a big 4 accountant you will need to be able to develop staff. Staff are the backbone of the big 4 accounting firms. The big 4 accounting firms have way more staff than any other position. You will have to be able to develop your staff in order to have a successful career. If you can't develop staff, your practice will not grow and you will be left doing the majority of the work.

Bad Answer

<u>An example of a bad answer to this question would be:</u>

I once had a group member in school who struggled to understand the basic accounting concepts in our accounting class. I knew the person was going to take some time to understand the concepts, so I just ended up doing their work for them so that we could finish the project in a timely manner.

Taking over for the group member helped us get a good grade.

<u>Why this is a bad answer</u>:

Even though you show that your group member has room for development, you don't really show the steps you took to develop them. You don't show that you were interested in developing them. For this question, you have to show willingness to understand another person's weaknesses, and the desire to help them.

Good Answer

<u>An example of a good answer to this question would be</u>:

I once had a classmate in my tax research class ask me how to get better at tax research. I helped them understand what skills and knowledge to strengthen by asking them a series of questions. I asked them if they knew hierarchy of authority in tax research, and I also asked them where they started once they received a research topic. By understanding the person's approach and current knowledge, I was able to develop a plan for them to improve their skills.

<u>Why this is a good answer</u>:

This shows how you assessed another person's skills and helped them improve. You asked questions to assess their current skillset, and then implemented a plan to improve upon those skills. That is exactly what the big 4 are looking for in a candidate. If you can show this as an entry level candidate, you are already ahead of most of your peers.

Interview Question 28

Give me an example of feedback or coaching you gave

someone who was having difficulty with an assignment.

Why do they ask this question?

The big 4 want to see if you are able to coach people in tough situations. Can you coach those individuals that inherently struggle with assignments? Can you coach people that are smart but struggle in certain areas? You need to show that you are able to coach people in many different situations in order to have success in the big 4 firms.

Bad Answer

An example of a bad answer to this question would be:

I once had a person in a group project who didn't have a good attitude about working. I told them they needed to improve their attitude because it was dragging down the performance of the group. I provided them real-time feedback. I like being open and honest and telling it how it is.

Why this is a bad answer:

This is a bad answer because "telling it like it is" is not really feedback, and this is where many people get it wrong in the big 4. All of the big 4 are very big about providing "honest" and "timely" feedback, but don't let that trap you. You still have to play politics. You can't just slam someone who is lazy to their face. You need to provide feedback, but you also need to be careful about how you word it and when you provide it.

Good Answer

An example of a good answer to this question would be:

I once had a group member who had a really bad attitude during a group project, so I took the person aside and spoke to them. I told them that they seemed disinterested in the work, and I asked if there was something bothering them.

It turns out that there was something bothering them. They had just failed a project in another class and that is what was affecting them. The group member apologized to me because they weren't aware that they were coming off as disinterested. In this case I was able to provide the feedback in an appropriate manner without embarrassing or offending my group member.

<u>Why this is a good answer</u>:

This is a good answer because it shows how you provided feedback in a tasteful and appropriate manner. You took the person aside and had a personal conversation. You also were not harsh to the person's face.

Interview Question 29

Give me an example of having received feedback or guidance and how you put the information to use.

Why do they ask this question?

The big 4 ask this question because they want to see how perceptive you are to feedback. Are you able to receive feedback without taking it personally?
Can you take feedback and improve on it, or does it go in one ear and out the other?

Bad Answer

<u>An example of a bad answer to this question would be:</u>

One of my prior bosses told me that I was too ambitious and that I didn't need to work so hard. I hear that a lot actually --- that I work too hard.

Why this is a bad answer:

Don't say this in an interview. This is a very typical answer. Nobody like someone that tries to show off by saying that their biggest weakness is working too hard. Just think of a couple of examples where you've received constructive feedback and use those. Do not say your one weakness is that you work too hard or care too much though.

Good Answer

An example of a good answer to this question would be:

After a project in school that involved public speaking, I received some feedback from the professor that I was monotoned and slumped over. It was hard for me to take the feedback at first, but I knew that improving my public speaking is key to my success in business. I took the professor's advice, and I also started attending toastmasters to improve my public speaking. After taking the feedback and analyzing it, I performed very well on my next public speaking project I had in school.

Why this is a good answer:

This is a good answer because it highlights not only your ability to take feedback but to also improve on that feedback. This candidate not only received the feedback from the professor, but they also improved their performance in the future by taking the professors feedback positively.

CHAPTER ELEVEN
Are You Afraid of Communication?

Can you communicate effectively? This is an area that is essential in the big 4. It is probably because many people don't communicate effectively in business or in personal life. Why do you think the big 4 get sued so often? It's because people don't communicate effectively. Someone on the engagement didn't communicate roles and responsibilities effectively. Maybe the audit team didn't communicate audit work performed in their workpapers. Maybe the client didn't communicate the operations of the business effectively in the financial statements. You must communicate effectively to be successful at the big 4, in life and in business. The big 4 will want you to demonstrate the following abilities to show that you can communicate:

- Can you organize your communication - Do you clarify the purpose and importance of your communication effectively?
- Can you comprehend communication from others - Do you actively listen and interpret messages from others?
- Do you ensure understanding - Do you seek input from your audience to make sure they understand your message?
- Do you speak confidently - Can you speak and write with a self-assured tone?
- Do you display professional demeanor - Can you exhibit

a calm and confident appearance without appearing nervous?

Interview Question 30

Tell me about a time when you had to modify your writing style to reach different audiences. How did you do it?

Why do they ask this question?

Now we've reached the section about communicating well. The big 4 would ask this question because they want to make sure that you can communicate effectively. You will not be doing too much public speaking your first couple of years, so it's important that your writing skills are good. You might not even be talking to clients that much other than through email. Therefore, you have to be able to communicate through writing. There are many different forms of writing communication as well.

You will have to be able to draft emails that are appropriate and don't offend people. There are internal emails and emails to clients. Many people send emails that are way too long and should be replaced by a simple phone call instead. There is also technical writing that has to be more professional and thought out than an email. Additionally, there is writing that you will have to do at performance review time that will be different than your email correspondence and technical writing.

Bad Answer

An example of a bad answer to this question would be:

The one example where I've had to modify my writing is for

school. The writing that I do in my college coursework is more professional than my other writing.

<u>Why this is a bad answer</u>:

You can't just say that you've written in different formats. You need to provide examples of why you've had to communicate differently in each format, and provide examples of how you considered your audience when you were writing it.

Good Answer

<u>An example of a good answer to this question would be</u>:

When I was applying for colleges, I had to modify my writing style depending on the school and the writing prompt. I had to be very professional for some schools and other schools were more informal. Additionally, I had to write differently than I had ever written before. A lot of my writing became historical. I was taking a look back at my life and writing about what I had accomplished and been through. I never completed that type of writing before the college application process.

<u>Why this is a good answer</u>:

This shows how you had to modify your writing style and write in a format that you had never written before. You also show how you considered your audience based on the school and prompt. You didn't just write the way you always wrote. You also did not write out of context. You considered the audience and wrote the way that you thought was the most appropriate to the situation.

Interview Question 31

Give me an example of a time when you had to persuade someone to do something solely through written communication. How did you persuade them?

Why do they ask this question?

Wow this is a tough question. Why would the big 4 ask this one? The primary reason that I think they ask this question is because email is a very common form of communication in the big 4. You will speak with your colleagues and clients through email. Some people are hard to get a hold of other than through email. There are plenty of big 4 professionals and clients that do not answer phones. They only read and respond to emails late at night. These are the people that you will have to reach through writing effectively.

Bad Answer

An example of a bad answer to this question would be:

I once had a project in school that had to be completed through only written communication. There was no other option than completing the assignment through writing.

Why this is a bad answer:

This question should not be answered by something you were forced to do. The question also asks for how you convinced someone through writing, so you don't want to provide an example of how you convinced a teacher to give you a good grade by completing your writing assignment. You want to show how you either completed this written task voluntarily or to ask permission for something.

Good Answer

<u>An example of a good answer to this question would be</u>:

There was a scholarship that I really wanted to apply for that required me to read a controversial book and convince them that one of the characters was morally correct. This was a very challenging project because the character was very controversial and seen as morally corrupt in most reviews of the book. My task was to convince the scholarship committee that this person was a good person only through writing. This really challenged me because you couldn't show your passion in person. You had to show your arguments through written word, and the facts didn't support your case. Because the facts weren't necessarily in my favor, I couldn't write from a matter-of-fact perspective. I had to become a very creative writer.

<u>Why this is a good answer</u>:

This is a good answer because it shows you how you had to convince the scholarship committee through writing only. It also shows that you took on a challenge independently and that challenge was to convince someone through only written communication. This fits the bill exactly.

Interview Question 32

Tell me about a time when you were successful in a negotiation. What did you do that made you successful?

Why do they ask this question?

You have to be able to negotiate to be successful in business. You will have to negotiate a lot in the big 4 as well.

More specifically you will have to negotiate with clients on bills and proposals. There will be times where clients don't agree with something you bill them for, and they will want you to write it off. You can't always write off what clients want you to because it is bad business. You have to be willing to negotiate sometimes.

There will also be times that you have to negotiate when you are trying to win work. You will have to negotiate fees, services and scope. Clients will want the lowest fee possible for the most amount of services. Internally leadership will want the most fees with the fewest services rendered. You will have to negotiate with both parties to make sure that they are happy.

Bad Answer

An example of a bad answer to this question would be:

I was shopping for a shirt recently at a boutique shop and negotiated the price of a shirt down at the counter.

Why this is a bad answer:

Negotiating a price down on a shirt or retail item alone is not going to be enough to impress a big 4 professional. You are going to need to show more skills or be a lot more illustrative.

Good Answer

An example of a good answer to this question would be:

I recently went on a vacation where I negotiated part of our activities. I really like scuba diving and knew that I wanted to scuba dive for a number dives. I also wanted one of my friends to join us on the boat who couldn't scuba dive. Since I was going to be enjoying so many activities with this scuba company, I tried negotiating some free scuba dives and a free day of snorkeling for my friend. The scuba company pushed back at first because they said that they normally don't negotiate.

After explaining the amount of value I was bringing to their company, they decided to give me the extra dives and free snorkel day for my friend. They did this because of the money I was going to spend and because I told them about how we would be providing them with good online reviews as well.

Why this is a good answer:

This is exactly the kind of negotiating the big 4 want to see. They want to see you having a back and forth. They also want to see you highlight what you bring to the table and using that to ask for more. You will often have to tell your clients that you are bringing value and even taking a hit in order to satisfy them.

This example also shows how you are bringing even more value than initially negotiated by telling the scuba company that you will provide a good review. In negotiations with clients, you sometimes have to get creative like that and come up with additional value adds that the client might not be considering.

CHAPTER TWELVE
Questions to Ask Big 4 Partner or Recruiter

There are many questions that you can ask a big 4 partner or recruiter. There are standard questions that you can ask such as:

- What is the worklife balance like?

- What is the firm's current stance and initiatives towards diversity?

- How is feedback provided to people in the group?

- What is the first thing that you would like me to contribute to the group if I joined today?

- What is your vision for the group for the future?

- There are also other questions that will make you seem a little more sophisticated and prepared if you ask them. Those questions are below.

Questions for recruiters

The following questions are questions you can ask your big 4 recruiter.

- What would you say the culture is like at this big 4 firm versus other big 4?

- I recently saw a news story about (fill in the blank headline about the firm) what is the firm doing to address that issue?

- What group and line of service will I be assigned to?

- Do you have a list of expectations for me as an associate/intern?

Questions for managers/partners

The following are questions that you can ask managers and partners of the big four. The questions that you ask them should be more focused towards big 4 client work and group specifics. You shouldn't ask them logistics questions like how much you will be earning or how long the internship will last.

- What values are important to you and your big 4 firm?

- What advice would you recommend to me that you wish you implemented early on in your career?

- Worklife balance is important to me as a young professional. What initiatives does your firm offer as far as worklife balance?

- What have you done to grow your personal and professional networks that I could implement today?

- What distinguishes this big 4 firm from other big 4 firms?

- Can you describe how you coached a new team member to successfully perform a challenging aspect of his/her job.

Printed in Great Britain
by Amazon